G

A Pilgrim's Companion

by
David Baldwin

For all those who come to this place seeking the Truth:
know that *"The truth will set you free,"* Jn 8:32

*All booklets are published thanks to the
generous support of the members of the
Catholic Truth Society*

CATHOLIC TRUTH SOCIETY
PUBLISHERS TO THE HOLY SEE

Contents

Grateful thanks to:
Right Reverend Dom Aidan Bellenger
Right Reverend Dom Charles Fitzgerald-Lombard
Reverend PJ Knox-Lecky
Doctor TF Hopkinson-Ball

All rights reserved. First published 2013 by The Incorporated Catholic Truth Society, 40-46 Harleyford Road London SE11 5AY Tel: 020 7640 0042 Fax: 020 7640 0046. Copyright © 2013 The Incorporated Catholic Truth Society.

ISBN 978 1 86082 880 5

Inside images: Page 17: *Glastonbury Tor at sunset*, iStock photos © charliebishop; Page 25: *Glastonbury Abbey - The Lady Chapel*, Shutterstock © Stephen Inglis; Page 34: *Youth 2000 Mass in the Lady Chapel crypt* © Kim Woolmer; Page 38: *Abbey model* © Glastonbury Abbey; Page 45: *The convent stable - the first Parish Church* © Former parishioner Mr GA Wheeler; Page 50: *Benediction at the Shrine* © Kim Woolmer; Page 62, *Walking routes of the Tor*, reproduced with permission of Glastonbury Abbey.

Foreword

Glastonbury is indeed special. The origins of the great Abbey and attendant Town are shrouded in the mists of time. Legend assigns St Patrick, and history St Dunstan, among others, to the Abbey's long list of distinguished abbots. Yet all things pass away, and not even the Abbey at the height of its prestige could resist the forces of greed that overran it in 1539.

The Town, of course, survived, and in one sense the Abbey with it. We have come a long way from the scorn of an age when anyone could cart away the stones at sixpence a load, to its current status as one of the foremost sites of our spiritual and cultural heritage - impressively presented and immaculately maintained. And this turbulent past is powerfully linked with the peaceful presence of the Restored Shrine of Our Lady St Mary of Glastonbury, and the other Christian sites around the town.

This welcome *Pilgrim's Companion* is much more than a guide. The tenth in David Baldwin's series on Christian Shrines, it manages to combine a poetic, almost mystical narrative, beautifully encapsulating the spirit of the place, with a minimum of tourists' directives, ensuring that the pilgrim neither loses the way nor misses the point.

However dampened by cold twenty-first century rationality, most of us acknowledge a deep-down ember of spirituality awaiting some gentle breath to reignite it. Glastonbury, with its rich Christian heritage, has the power to bestow that breath.

This great Abbey - past, present and into the future - is the sort of place of which Jacob famously exclaimed:

"Surely this is none other than the House of God and the Gate of Heaven."

Gn 28:17

The Right Reverend Dom Charles Fitzgerald-Lombard
Titular Abbot of Glastonbury,
March 2013

Glastonbury

A casual reckoning of Glastonbury's population - approximately 9,000 - coupled with its location deep in rural Somerset, would probably invoke a generalised image of a small, quiet, country market town - akin to many others throughout the land - quietly going about the usual daily business connected with its rural surrounds.

However, first-time visitors to Glastonbury, wandering down the High Street and taking in the variety and range of colourful New Age and 'alternative' shops, may immediately start thinking otherwise. But in contrast to all this, they will also come across, within short distances around the town, a substantial and elegant fifteenth century Anglican church, the dignified ruins of a huge and once beautiful Abbey set in spacious and tranquil grounds, an internationally renowned Roman Catholic Shrine just opposite, and, on looking up to the near easterly skyline, the prominent, iconic hill feature of Glastonbury Tor.

They may then start to realise that what they see about them - whilst also taking in the happenings of many previous centuries - is that Glastonbury is no ordinary rural town, but one with several intriguing stories to tell. These are stories that interweave myth, mystique, legend, tradition and historicity - sometimes dubbed as 'mythtory' - all intermingling and blurring, so as to beguile, bemuse and bedazzle - so, beware! And all of it has a romance about it: Joseph of Arimathea, the Holy Thorn, the Holy Grail, King Arthur, the Isle of Avalon, saintly pilgrims, the anguish of Dissolution and Reformation, spiritual forces and ley lines, the reality of brutal martyrdom, New Age practices and beliefs - but all of that is just grist to the mill in and around Glastonbury.

These tales continue to actively attract many thousands of people every year, all seeking some spiritual truth - to define, confirm, affirm, clarify - hoping to find and follow whatever strand that brought them here, and attempting to untwist it from the others.

The strongest of these strands, and one that has endured over the last two millennia, is that of Christianity in Glastonbury, bringing over those hundreds of years, and continuing to this day, countless pilgrims, all on their individual journey as they seek to inform and strengthen their faith.

This is the strand that we will follow in this small book. Its purpose is to set the 'Glastonbury scene' and accompany the pilgrim through the principal places of Christian and historical interest in the town, with relevant prayers and meditations along the way. For there is certainly a good day's worth of 'gentle pilgrimaging' in and around the town; a visit to take in and pray or attend Mass at the

Restored Shrine of Our Lady St Mary of Glastonbury; a gentle wander round the tranquil and beautifully maintained grounds of the Abbey; prayer and reflection in the glorious Anglican church of St John the Baptist; and, if weather, time and energy beckon, a good blow up the Tor, which affords fantastic views, but is also a place of sombre reflection. Other places will also be pointed out - in the town and a bit further afield.

A book of this limited size can but only scratch the surface of this intriguing place. Hopefully this may only serve to stimulate rather than frustrate. But at its heart are the relevant prayers and meditations which are offered at each major stopping-off point, and these, joining with your own prayers, should serve to sustain you on this leg of your pilgrim journey.

> "Yahweh says this, 'Stand at the crossroads and look, ask for the ancient paths: which was the good way? Take it and you will find rest for yourselves."
>
> *Jr* 6:16

Setting the Scene

"The Town's history and legends, embracing the coming of Christianity to Britain, the stories of King Arthur and the mysteries of the Holy Grail, are topics that have haunted the British imagination for centuries."

WJ Keith *American academic*

The compact, rural town of Glastonbury is set in the low-lying Levels and Moors of Somerset - 160,000 acres of wide-horizoned flatlands, given mainly to pasture, willow trees and peat diggings, extending from the Somerset coastline some sixteen miles away. The town is twenty-three miles south of Bristol; the nearest city is the one claimed as the smallest in England: the lovely cathedral town of Wells, six miles away. Nearby is the popular 'factory shopping' town of Street - claimed as the biggest village in England, as it is still governed by a parish council.

Early times

Evidence from ancient, well-preserved timber trackway, built in the thirty-ninth century BC, and laid in a network across the surrounding marshes, shows signs of human habitation from those distant Neolithic times, and ever since. During those centuries past, much of the low-lying area of the Levels was either permanently waterlogged or submerged by sea water. The name 'Somerset' itself indicates an area of 'summer pastures', with grazing animals having to be moved to higher ground during the floods of winter months. Several early settlements have been discovered on the natural 'islands' formed by the surrounding higher ground.

Subsequent draining of the Levels had been going on since before the Domesday Book. In the Middle Ages, the monks of Glastonbury Abbey were instrumental in contributing significantly to this huge, manual effort to increase their estates; drainage work continues extensively to this day. As a result, the land is symmetrically criss-crossed with large and small man-made drainage ditches, known locally as '*rhynes*' (pronounced 'reens').

The Levels are still prone to large-scale fresh water flooding, particularly during the winter rains. As a result, this wetlands setting provides an attractive, hugely bio-diverse area, dotted with Sites of Special Scientific Interest, Nature and Bird Reserves, and pre-historic sites. It is also a prime area to witness the amazing spectacle of the fabulous murmurations of hundreds of thousands of starlings in their huge formations as they wheel and dip against the setting sun, to their night roosts.

There is archaeological evidence, through a continuous pottery sequence found in and around Glastonbury Abbey, of human occupation stretching from the Late Iron Age, through Roman, sub-Roman and into Saxon periods, including high status wares in every period, suggesting that something out of the ordinary was happening on this site. The first historic records of the settlement at Glastonbury appear in the seventh century, referring to it as '*Glestingaburg*', one possible meaning being 'monastic enclosure'. For it is in Glastonbury that the strand that we are following - that of Christianity - goes back to its very earliest times.

Joseph of Arimathea

Legend: a non-historical or unverifiable story handed down by tradition from earlier times and popularly accepted as historical.

Tradition: the handing down of statements, beliefs, legends, customs, information from generation to generation, especially by word of mouth or by practice.

www.dictionaryreference.com

And those earliest times start with Joseph of Arimathea, the man who laid Jesus's body in his own tomb. Although the timeline of the legend of Joseph in Glastonbury goes back to even pre-crucifixion days, the first record of any such connection emerges from a thirteenth century scribing monk of Glastonbury Abbey, writing about St Philip evangelising in France in the first century:

> "Desiring to spread the word of Christ further, he [Philip] sent twelve of his disciples into Britain to teach the word of life. It is said that he appointed as their leader, his very dear friend Joseph of Arimathea, who had buried the Lord. They came to Britain in AD 63, the

fifteenth year after the assumption of the Blessed Mary, and confidently began to preach the faith of Christ." "[Soon after which] the saints were incited by a vision of the Archangel Gabriel to build a church in honour of the Virgin Mary...making the lower part of all of its walls of twisted wattle, an unsightly construction no doubt, but one adorned by God with many miracles."

Here was the first documented evidence firmly anchoring Joseph to Glastonbury, as the monks sought to formalise and establish the identity of the founder of their ancient church and monastery - a founder with the highly desired sub-apostolic status required for such a prestigious establishment.

This mediaeval legend developed further, with Joseph bringing two sacred cruets to Glastonbury, one containing Christ's blood and the other his sweat, collected from the crucifixion. This was the precursor of the later Holy Grail legend, which now predominates.

Of the pre-crucifixion legend, this tells of Joseph, reputedly a trader in tin and lead, and in pursuit of his business travelling up through Europe to the mining areas of Cornwall and Somerset, bringing with him his great-nephew, the boy Jesus to Glastonbury. This legend did not surface until after the sixteenth century, and went on to be acclaimed in William Blake's early nineteenth century poem, subsequently set to Parry's music, as the stirring, mystical hymn 'Jerusalem':

"And did those feet in ancient time
Walk upon England's mountains green?
And was the holy Lamb of God
On England's pleasant pastures seen?"

The Glastonbury Holy Thorn

Similarly, the existence of the Holy Thorn, so inextricably linked with Glastonbury, was not evident until the early sixteenth century, where the earliest literary reference was of:

"Three hawthorns also, that groweth in Werall,
Do burge and bear green leaves at Christmas
As fresh as other in May....",

and, at that time, without any reference linking them to Joseph. Nonetheless, the legend that emerged subsequently, tells of Joseph resting on Wearyall Hill ('*Werall*'), the feature just west of Glastonbury Tor, planting his walking staff in the ground, where overnight it took root and blossomed into a thorn tree. This was the miracle that was supposed to have convinced the local pagan community of the power of God, and the start of Christian conversion. To this day, a thorn tree grows on this hill, but has had a very checkered history. Although other copies existed (and still do) around Glastonbury, the 'original' thorn on Wearyall was cut down in 1653 during the English Civil War to combat superstition. A cutting from the original was planted back on the hill in 1951, but sadly it was seriously vandalised in 2010, and has since been replaced.

Although a common hawthorn, it is said to be of Middle Eastern origin, and unusually flowers twice a year, at Christmas and May. Since the 1920s a charming tradition has existed of sending a flowering sprig to adorn the monarch's Christmas breakfast table, the sprig being ceremonially cut from the tree in St John's churchyard.

But, whatever its provenance, to the Christian, the Holy Thorn serves as a stark reminder of the inglorious crown of the King of Kings.

The first church

In continuing the strand of early Christian arrival in the area, tradition tells of a simple church of wattle and daub, *vetusta ecclesia* or *lignea basilica*, dedicated to the Virgin Mary being built (or renewed) by missionaries sent from Rome at the behest of King Saint Lucius, King of the Britons, traditionally credited with bringing Christianity to England in the second century. Here, from this 'Old Church', started, or continued, the small monastic community, whose successors were subsequently and reputedly joined by St Patrick, who came from Ireland in 433, taking on the abbacy, and remaining until his death.

These could be the first early intimations of Glastonbury becoming a site of Marian devotion in England - perpetuated to this day by the current parish church and Shrine being dedicated to 'Our Lady St Mary of Glastonbury', and maintaining the claim that it is the oldest Shrine to Our Lady north of the Alps.

The story now starts taking on a bit more substance with early historical fragments: an allusion in the sixth century to a monastic church at *Ynyswitrin*, one of the putative Celtic names given to the Glastonbury premonitory, where 'the *Genetrix* was venerated'; in 681 reference to a land grant by the West Saxon sub-king Baldred to 'the church of blessed Mary and blessed Patrick'.

This is all evidence of seventh century Somerset having been conquered and occupied by the Saxons, who had converted to Christianity. A significant development is that given in 704 by the Charter of King Ine of Wessex, recognising the monastic community and granting lands 'of St Mary of Glastonbury'. Following this, and under Ine's patronage, the first stone church, dedicated to Ss Peter and Paul was built around 712. It was built to the east of the still-existing Old Church of Our Lady, which by now may have been reconstructed in timber.

The earliest surviving written account of any substance, and linking all the above together, surfaces around 1000 from an unknown monk recording what was commonly believed about the Old Church of St Mary at this time:

"For it was in this island that, by God's guidance, the first novices of the catholic law discovered an ancient church, not built or dedicated in the memory of man. Later, the builder of the heavens himself revealed by many miraculous and supernatural happenings that it was consecrated to him and his holy Mother Mary. To this church they added a second, building it of stone and the bishops dedicated it to Christ and his apostle St Peter."

The detailed story of the Abbey's continuing fortunes will be taken up in the relevant chapter on the Abbey. What is clear though, is that the church and monastery, throughout the many centuries of its active life, were the *raison d'être* for Glastonbury's continuing existence and prospects. It was the hub around which the surrounding countryside and town survived and thrived: through the agricultural endeavours of its extensive estates, and the ever-present passing of countless pilgrims. Whilst the Abbey no longer looms large over the town, it still resonates with a powerful presence - physically, as dignified and lovingly maintained ruins in serene grounds, but spiritually, still charged with the presence of the countless prayers from the past, that whisper from down the centuries, drawing and inspiring today's seekers of Truth from all over the world.

"If you came this way,
Taking any route, starting from anywhere,
At any time or at any season,
It would always be the same: you would have to put off
Sense and notion. You are not here to verify,
Instruct yourself, or inform curiosity
Or carry report. You are here to kneel
Where prayer has been valid."

TS Eliot *Quartet No 4*

Arthur and the Isle of Avalon

The other mysterious and fascinating figure associated with Glastonbury is Arthur. "The fact of the matter is that there is no historical evidence about Arthur; we must reject him from our histories and, above all, from the titles of our books", is the blunt assertion of historian David Dumville. It is an assertion which has obviously gone completely unheeded, given the acres of books and writing on Arthur. But, because of the tantalising lack of any substantial, corroborated historical details, the story of this fifth/sixth century warrior king is mainly folklore, dashing legend and imaginative literary invention. However, with the mythology and mystique removed, it is claimed that there clearly did exist a Celtic prince or warlord round that time who led the defence of Britain against Saxon invaders.

Arthur's main link with Glastonbury, though, is more through his death than his life. It is recounted that after his many chivalrous exploits and deeds with his knights, he was wounded by the notorious traitor Mordred at the battle of Camlann in Somerset around 542. He was then taken 'across the waters' to the 'Isle of Avalon' to have his wounds tended. Here he died, and subsequent details relating to this are described in the chapter on the Abbey.

The descriptor 'Isle of Avalon' has long been associated with Glastonbury - from its early topography of being almost surrounded by water. Early names for Glastonbury come from the Welsh *Ynys Affalach* - Island of Apples (of

"…that ethereal vision of the mystical Isle of Avalon…"

which Somerset is a prolific producer), and its surrounds as *Ynis Gutrin* - Island of Glass. Other derivations link it with the Celtic demi-god Avalloc or Avallach. And indeed today, when viewing the Tor, particularly on a misty early morning or bright moonlit night, and when floods are at their height with all surrounding fields completely submerged, one can quite readily conjure up that ethereal vision of the mystical Isle of Avalon….

Dissolution and beyond

After the Dissolution of the Monasteries, the estates belonging to the Abbey were either seized by the Crown, or sold or passed to other landlords, and the coherent output of the Abbey's estates fragmented and diluted. The Abbey buildings provided a ready-made 'quarry', being dismantled for local building projects. However, unusually, the Lady Chapel was largely untouched, and can be seen today much as it was left in the late sixteenth century. It is one of the few Lady chapels that survived the Dissolution, one which had already, for so long, in some form, stood in veneration of the Virgin Mary. Catholicism was driven underground; the story of its re-emergence is taken up in the Chapter of the Restored Shrine of Our Lady of Glastonbury.

After the shockwaves of the abrupt closure of the Abbey - the effect akin to a modern-day closure of a major local industry - the town and area had to realign with new owners, new opportunities: either held in the traditional workings of the land - livestock, dairy, apples, or through other nascent trades, such as cloth manufacture and retail, and tanning and associated activities, particularly wool and sheepskin.

The Town remained a centre for the wool trade until the late eighteenth century, but the opening of the Glastonbury canal in 1833 stimulated increased volumes of other forms of commerce and development. However, with the arrival of the railways in the 1850s, the canal's utility was soon eclipsed, and the railway continued to service the industries of Glastonbury, until its closure in 1966.

Although rural life and local industry still goes on in and around the town, the nineteenth and twentieth centuries have seen tourism and leisure developing as an economic mainstay, through a growing awareness of Glastonbury's mystical past, its related buildings, places and people, all drawing in those many seekers.

Glastonbury is twinned with two other mystical places, the first being the Greek island of Patmos, in which St John the Evangelist wrote the Book of Revelation in a cave. This twinning was sealed in March 2008, and because of their association with the two saints who knew Christ, is described as a 'Twinning in Perpetuity'. The other significant twinning, in 2007, is with Lalibela, Ethiopa's twelfth century capital, and an important ancient Christian pilgrimage site.

"Blessed are those who find their strength in you, whose hearts are set on pilgrimage."

Ps 84:5

The Abbey

"For my house will be called a house of prayer for all peoples."

Is 56:7

An historic midnight approaches - a midnight that will bring to a close the previous thousand years and open the next: it is the turn of the Millennium. In the floodlight ruins of the Great Abbey at Glastonbury, in the depths of that dark, flickering, flare-lit night, was an atmospheric and sizeable ecumenical gathering, jointly celebrating this momentous occasion, significant enough to be televised live by the BBC amongst all the secular celebrations around the nation. During this Millennium Service, the Titular Abbot of Glastonbury, an honorific title held by a former Abbot of the nearby Benedictine monastery of Downside, led the congregation and other clergy members in prayer:

"Lord of Creation, Giver of Peace, in whose power are all times and seasons, and in whose hands lies the destiny of all the world, let not our hopes perish, nor our trust be in vain.

Give us grace to root out from our lives, the bitterness of ancient wrongs - and the desire to be avenged - for the betrayals of long ago. Save us from the tyranny of history, and grant us grace and courage to give and receive the forgiveness, which alone can heal the wounds which remain.

Set us free to serve each other, and to live the present moment as a gift of new life.

Bless this new year and century, and crown it with your goodness.

Keep us in your peace, grant us every blessing, and lead us to our Eternal Home, where you reign for all eternity."

Glastonbury's heart

The Abbey sits where it has always been - right in the heart of the Town, having once been its very heart. The graceful ruins are set in thirty-six acres of beautifully maintained Somerset parkland. As well as being able to get close-in amongst the ruins to wonder, or pray, or simply to try and catch those echoes of centuries ago, there are also plenty of quiet corners with benches under shady trees, or pathways to take a meditative meander, or maybe seek out the ideal spot for a picnic.

And in this perfect setting, one can contemplate and reflect on the remains of a noble, painstakingly and lovingly constructed architecture of another spiritual era, and what in today's context, they stand for. At the simplest level, this place provides welcome and refreshing respite in amongst the hubbub and hustle of our daily lives.

Access to the Abbey grounds is off Magdalene Street, under the arch by the Town Hall. A short alley leads past the well-stocked Abbey shop, up to the visitors' entrance. A visit to the Abbey's website will give details of how to get there, parking, entrance prices, seasonal opening times and other general practical information.

However, before we take that walk round the Abbey and its grounds, we can now catch up from where we left off in the introductory chapter - a story that is now well-documented.

St Dunstan

That first stone church, endowed by the Saxon King Ine of Wessex, was extended later on in the eighth century. In the ninth century came the Danes, whose incursions into Wessex despoiled the monastery, turning its fortunes to a low ebb. Then, into the Abbey's destiny steps the locally-born hermit monk, St Dunstan (c.909-988). In 943 he became Abbot, not only restoring the faltering religious life of the monastery by instituting the Benedictine Rule, but also physically enlarging Ine's church, as well as laying down one of the earliest cloistered arrangements for monastic buildings in England.

Dunstan went on to become Archbishop of Canterbury (960-78), serving several English kings as a minister of state. His feast day is celebrated on the 19th of May. He is the patron saint of blacksmiths and precious metal workers.

During that same period, King Edgar's patronage granted more lands and gifts of gold and silver, and the monastery was noted later on in the Domesday Book in 1086, as 'the wealthiest religious house in England'. Here also, in recognition of its standing, three Saxon Kings were buried: Edgar the Peaceful of England, Edmund I of England, and Edmund Ironside.

Rebuilding and the Great Fire

The coming of the Normans after 1066 brought many changes to the Abbey - heralding a major rebuild in the Norman style. Dunstan's huge, extended church was demolished in 1077 and replaced by a larger church. This church, in turn, was not considered fitting by a subsequent Abbot, who, in 1100 demolished it, building an even grander edifice, modelled on the great church of St Albans.

Just a few decades later tragedy struck, when on 25th May 1184, this great monastery, along with the Old Church and much of their treasures, were destroyed by fire. One item of note from the conflagration of the Old Church was the reported 'miraculous survival' of the wooden statue of Our Lady, which had for so long been venerated there, and which took on a profound new significance.

Under the patronage of Henry II (1133-89) re-building got underway almost immediately, and significantly, started with the construction of the Lady Chapel that still stands today. It owes its unusual position at the western extremity of the Abbey, as with some purpose and poignancy, it replaced the Old Church of St Mary in the same spot and to the exact dimensions. It continued to function as a discrete church, complete with a separate order of secular priests - the Clerks of Our Lady - created by the Abbot to serve the church and its many pilgrims.

In 1189 construction of the new great Abbey started at its east end, and by 1213 there was sufficient of the church for it to be put into use, being solemnly consecrated on Christmas Day. Building continued well on into the century, with the major work being completed in mid-thirteenth century with the west front and flanking, twin towers. This Great Church was of a scale and magnificence said to be second only in size and prestige to Westminster Abbey.

Arthur

We now need to resume the story of Arthur from the introductory chapter, where he was carried to Glastonbury, fatally wounded, around the year 542. It was said that he was buried in the Abbey's cemetery on the south side of the Lady Chapel. In 1191, a search of this site was instituted to find Arthur's remains, where reportedly, when the monks had dug down seven feet, they hit a large, flat stone, on the underside of which was attached a lead cross inscribed in Latin: *'Here lies Arthur buried in the island*

The Lady Chapel and Abbey ruins.

of Avalon'. On digging down further, they found a massive oak coffin which contained two bodies - one of a sizeable man, the other, of a woman, whose lengths of golden hair were still intact. The bodies were said to be Arthur's and his Queen, Guinevere's.

The destiny of these remains is told very simply on the metal plaque which you will find planted in the ground in the Choir of the Abbey, just in front of the High Altar:

"Site of King Arthur's Tomb. In the year 1191 the bodies of King Arthur and his Queen were said to have been found on the south side of the Lady Church. On 19th April 1278 their remains were removed in the presence of King Edward I and Queen Eleanor to a black marble tomb on this site. This tomb survived until the Dissolution of the Abbey in 1539".

Whatever the veracity of Arthur's existence, his very 'being' was regarded by the monks of the time as the perfect synthesis of the Christian ideal, and therefore worthy of emulation and veneration. Sadly, in the ensuing destruction wrought by the Dissolution, the whereabouts of these remains were lost to history.

After completion of the main construction, the internal architectural detailing and the decorating of the nave and chapels in rich, vibrant colours and style of the era would have continued on into the fourteenth century.

Dissolution and Reformation

By the early sixteenth century, there were more than 800 religious houses in Britain, populated by an estimated 10,000 monks and other religious. Following the Black Death, there was a general decline in the population in these houses, and in a few, the quality of spiritual character had been eroded by worldly activities, posing in some, the need for reform.

This period was the reign of Henry VIII, who, in attempting to solve his marital problems had broken from Rome, declaring himself the Supreme Head of the Church in England. And although the great majority of clerics throughout the land, including the Abbot of Glastonbury, had taken the Oath of Supremacy to Henry, he may still have felt threatened by the religious houses subverting his newly taken stand against Rome. Coupled with this, was the depletion of the national coffers through the failed wars against France. His elegant but devastating solution was to turn on the monasteries, on the pretext of purge and reform, but with more of an eye on their rich treasures.

This was the Dissolution of the Monasteries, which, when completed in 1540, left no functioning monastery or religious house in the land. The religious communities were summarily evicted, including the fifty or so monks of Glastonbury. Some were martyred. The lands and buildings were seized by the Crown and sold or leased to secular owners. The magnificent churches were despoiled, with statues, stained glass windows, paintings, and any other 'evidence of Rome', particularly Lady chapels and chantries, being summarily destroyed. That precious wooden statue of Our Lady, saved from the great fire, disappeared without trace, seemingly ending the presence and purpose of her Shrine in Glastonbury.

The end for the Glastonbury monastery was particularly brutal and explicit. The Abbot, Richard Whiting, now a frail old man, was subjected to a show trial, and found guilty of treason. On 15th of November 1539, he was tied to a hurdle and dragged in ignominy to the top of the Tor. There, with two of his fellow monks, Roger James and John Thorne, Whiting was hanged. In the customary manner of enforcing deterrence, his body was quartered, and displayed in Bath, Wells, Bridgwater and Ilchester. His head was placed over the Abbey gateway. Richard Whiting, noted by Cardinal Wolsley as, 'an upright and religious monk…commendable for his life, virtues and learning', was beatified by Pope Leo XIII in 1895, and his martyrdom, with his fellow monks, is commemorated locally at the Shrine of Our Lady of Glastonbury on 15th of November with Mass, followed by a commemorative walk by parishioners up the Tor.

Mary's Dowry

The Dissolution was but one aspect of the wide-ranging Reformation; another was the suppression of the hitherto strong Marian cult in England. This cult was epitomised by England being depicted as 'Mary's Dowry', with a fourteenth century Archbishop referring specifically to, "We English, being her own Dowry, as we are commonly called, aught to surpass others in fervour of our praises and devotions". Although the provenance of the 'Dowry' cachet has never been traced, it is worth speculating that the early Marian devotion evident in Glastonbury may have played some part in spreading it throughout the land.

But as far as the Dissolution went, "… monasticism and the cult of Mary fell together, just as they had stood together during the preceding Catholic centuries." However, as one author has observed, "Although the Reformation had swept away the material expressions of the Virgin's presence" - her sanctuaries, shrines and statues - the people of this land, "have retained in their hearts the indelible memory that they are her special inheritance".

In the decades after Henry, the primacy of Catholicism and Protestantism swung back and forth, incurring on both sides violence, bloodshed, division and bitterness. The prevailing effect of the Reformation in Europe, now widespread, was also being brought to Britain, with the exported theologies and practices of Protestantism being instituted. Over the next centuries, and as Catholics remained to be seen as a political threat to the Crown or to the newly established Anglican Church, they were in effect driven underground, either through discrimination, active persecution, or sometimes execution, as witnessed by the forty Martyrs of England and Wales, who between 1535 and 1679, were put to death for 'treason'. Their feast day is celebrated on 4th May.

In 1767 it was estimated that the Catholic population in England was about 1%, and attitudes began to soften. Catholic worship was legalised in 1791, followed by the watershed Roman Catholic Relief Act of 1829, the culmination of Catholic Emancipation in Britain, and resulting in the formal restoration of the Catholic hierarchy by Pope Pius IX in 1850. What effect this all had on Glastonbury, will be taken up in the chapter on the Restored Shrine of Our Lady of Glastonbury.

"Forgive…"

"Pardon your neighbour any wrongs done to you, and when you pray, your sins will be forgiven. If anyone nurses anger against another, can one then demand compassion from the Lord? Showing no pity for someone like oneself, can one then plead for one's own sins?"

Si 28:2-4

"Unity…"

"Priority on the ecumenical path to unity should undoubtedly be given to prayer in common, to the mutual bond in prayer of all those who unite together around Christ himself. If Christians succeed, regardless of their divisions, to unite together more and more in common prayer around Christ, then their awareness will grow that what divides them, compared with what unites them, is small indeed."

Blessed Pope John Paul II

Prayer for Christian Unity

"Heavenly Father,
You have called us in the body of your Son Jesus Christ
To continue his work of reconciliation
And reveal you to the world:
Forgive us the sins that tear us apart;
Give us the courage to overcome our fears
And to seek that **unity** which is your gift and your will;
Through Jesus Christ your Son our Lord,
Who is alive and reigns with you,
In the unity of the Holy Spirit,
One God, now and forever."

Prayer written for 2010 Papal visit to UK

The Abbey awakes

And in the meantime, since that violent upheaval, 'this great, broken Abbey slept', passing through many hands, with the ruins becoming more dilapidated and the grounds completely overgrown.

In 1908 the sleeping Abbey was gently awakened, when the grounds were purchased by a trust on behalf of the Church of England. Over the next years the undergrowth was tamed, the ruins stripped of vegetation, archaeological investigations undertaken, and restoration work commenced, which is significant and ongoing to this day.

As you pass through the entrance area you will see the visitors' centre and museum. It is a modern, well-presented and informative aspect of your Abbey visit. Have a good browse round at some stage, and do have a look at the beautiful scaled and detailed model showing how this glorious church looked just before the Dissolution.

Meditating and praying round the Abbey

The first building you will encounter on leaving the ticket lobby at the rear is the small, roofed and whitewashed chapel of St Patrick. The chapel was built in 1512 to serve the nearby almshouses. It has recently been completely refurbished, with inside, the colourful, vivid pre-Reformation-style frescoes decorating the walls, all telling the stories of people associated with Glastonbury and the Abbey. It is regularly used for worship, and is a lovely quiet spot to pray and reflect.

Immediately behind the chapel grows one of the Holy Thorns. Then, as you look towards the ruins, you will see a prominent, stark wooden cross close by, on which the plaque says, "The Cross. The symbol of our Faith. The Gift of Queen Elizabeth II marks a Christian Sanctuary, so ancient that only legend can record its origin".

From here there is no set route to your wanderings. Every location of interest either has a display board or a metal plaque, explaining its significance.

The Lady Chapel

Maybe you will head to the Lady Chapel, which is closest. This elegant structure is unusually built in the distinct Romanesque style, possibly to maintain a similarity and connection to the Old Church during a period when Gothic architecture was taking hold in Britain. You will notice the elaborately sculptured Biblical scenes in concentric rows round the entrance archways.

Inside, you can view the whole chapel from the ramp and take in the helpful explanations on the display boards. The open, crypt chapel of St Joseph of Arimathea is below. The physical co-location of these two chapels gives rise to the powerful evocation of the mystery of the Christian cycle of *life-death-life*: above, the altar of the chapel to Mary, from whose womb came the Christ Child into the world; directly below it, the altar of St Joseph of Arimathea, into whose tomb the dead Christ was laid, and from where he

Youth 2000 Mass in the Lady Chapel crypt.

rose back to life. There is an ancient well in the crypt. This chapel is used on occasions for worship and Masses.

Rosary recommendation: The Glorious Mysteries: The Resurrection, the Ascension, the Descent of the Holy Spirit, the Assumption, and the Crowning of Our Lady. If time or circumstance preclude, just pray the third decade, as here in this chapel the great event of Pentecost, at which Our Lady was present, was celebrated for many hundreds of years.

Hymn to Mary

"From east to west, from shore to shore,
Let every heart awake and sing.
The holy Child, whom Mary bore,
The Christ, the everlasting King.
Behold, the world's Creator wears,
The form and fashion of a slave,
Our very flesh our maker shares,
His fallen creature, Man, to save.
For this how wondrously he wrought,
A Maiden, in her lowly place,
Became in ways beyond all thought,
the chosen vessel of his grace.
She bowed her to the Angel's word,
declaring what the Father willed,
And suddenly the promised Lord,
that pure and hallowed temple filled...."

From a fifth century Latin hymn by Irish hymnographer

Coelius Sedulius, the earliest known hymn to have been composed in her honour in the Western Church.

As you exit out the other (south) side, just look immediately left, at eye level, on the exterior wall. Here you will see faintly inscribed 'IESUS MARIA'. I confess this small inscription is one of my most favourite 'Abbey moments'. For here, those many hundreds of years ago, an unknown stonemason carved these simple but elegant letters, expressing that profound eternal relationship between Son and Mother, one that is echoed in the same manner in the nearby Shrine of Our Lady. You will also notice that the elaborate carvings round the arch of this exit cease abruptly - for what reason is not known....

The Great Abbey

"Bare ruined choirs where late the sweet birds sing."
                                    Shakespeare, *Sonnet 73*

You may now be moving on up to the main part of the Abbey, passing the Galilee, which linked the hitherto separate church to Our Lady to the Abbey, thus formally creating the Abbey's Lady Chapel.

It is difficult to imagine the size and scope of this great building just from these vestiges, but the two massive columns at the entrance to the Choir, reaching and arching emptily upwards - and the indicated floor plan extending around you, may give a faint flicker - and this is where you can refer to the picture on the following page of how the Abbey once looked. Then, you can start to wonder at the immensity of it all; the ingenuity, skill and dedication of those who conceived, built and ran this holy place. But above all, you can reflect on those countless thousands who came here before you, from centuries ago until now, to worship, pray or just be here, expressing their hopes, joys, desires, disasters, sorrows - as you may feel moved to do:

> "That which was wasted will be restored
> as Love gives love.
> Man cannot hasten that will be
> except by prayer,
> true prayer in union with Love's creation
> to build afresh
> that which man's folly did break and mar
> in pride of self.
> Love flows in healing
> with every prayer that is of truth
> when self is given
> in abandonment
> that Love may rule…"
>
> from 'Glastonbury', a rhythmic prayer
> by Gilbert Shaw (1886-1967)

Moving on up through the Nave, past the Transept chapels left and right, into the Choir or Sanctuary, where Arthur and Guinevere were said to be entombed in front of the

The Abbey, just before Dissolution.

High Altar. Lastly, at the east end, behind the High Altar, is the small chapel of St Edgar. Beyond and above that, over the hedge, you can see the substantial nineteenth century buildings of Abbey House, a retreat centre run by the Diocese of Bath and Wells.

> **Rosary recommendation:** As you wander the grounds you may wish to pray the Mysteries of Light: The Baptism of the Lord, the Wedding of Cana, the Proclamation of the Kingdom, the Transfiguration, the Institution of the Eucharist. If time or circumstance preclude, you could pray the third decade in the nave and choir, recalling that from this very place the Gospel was publicly proclaimed.

Peaceful grounds

Pathways will lead you up to the wildlife area, complete with active badger sett, to the duck pond, down to the fish pond, and through the orchard and small herbal garden. Back closer to the Abbey you can examine the bare outlines of the Cloister garden, the monks' accommodation and Refectory area. Back just beyond the Lady Chapel, a small plaque indicates the location of the ancient cemetery, of which now there is no visible evidence.

The last building, set some way from the monastery, is the distinctive, conical-roofed Abbot's Kitchen. This fourteenth century octagonal building is one of the best preserved mediaeval kitchens in Europe, and inside, its function of providing sumptuous meals for the Abbot and his many visitors and guests is plain to see. Close by, is the mere stump of the south west angle of the sizeable Abbot's Hall.

An outdoor café is open during the summer season. The Abbey stages many varied events throughout the year, including the two major Christian pilgrimages - Roman Catholic and Anglican. Full details are on the Abbey website.

As you come to the end of your visit to the Abbey, you may wish to return to that Millennium Prayer at the head of this chapter, and reflect on it, particularly the sentence, "Set us free to serve each other, and to live the present moment as a gift of new life…", before you step out on your pilgrim journey again.

"…no longer strangers…"

"So you are no longer aliens or foreign visitors; you are fellow-citizens with the holy people of God and part of God's household. You are built upon the foundations of the apostles and prophets, and Christ Jesus himself is the cornerstone. Every structure knit together in him grows into a holy temple in the Lord; and you too, in him, are being built up into a dwelling-place of God in the Spirit."

Ep 2:19-22

"How good, how delightful it is to live as brothers all together!"

Ps 133:1

The Restored Shrine of Our Lady of Glastonbury

"A Shrine is traditionally a place of pilgrimage, and reminds us, in an earthly way, of our spiritual journey of faith. Through Baptism we embark on a road that is sometimes smooth, sometimes rough, but we do not journey alone. As Christians we have our eyes firmly fixed upon the Kingdom of God, as revealed by our Lord and Saviour, Jesus Christ. The message of Our Lady, His Mother, is a simple one. In Jn 2:5 she points to her Son, and says: "Do whatever He tells you." And so, it is in this Shrine, that we worship God and give honour to the *Theotokos*, the God-bearer. She is the prototype of the Church, in that she gives us an example of discipleship unparalleled in the history of salvation. She is humble and courageous, obedient and strong, maternal and virginal, constantly directing us towards her Son."

Fr Kevin Knox-Lecky,
Parish Priest of Glastonbury, 1999-2012

Restoration of Catholicism

As Catholicism cautiously re-emerged in this country in the late eighteenth and early nineteenth century, vividly described by Newman as, '*a gens lucifuga*', a 'people who shunned the light', "found in corners and alleys and cellars and the housetops, or in the recesses of the country". None more so was the case in Glastonbury, where a Town historian observed of 1780, "there were reputed papists in the parish".

The momentum for the restoration of Catholicism in and around Glastonbury came from a most unlikely direction: France. Amongst the many orders fleeing the religious persecutions and anti-clerical regimes of the late nineteenth and early twentieth centuries, were the Missionaries of the Sacred Heart who established themselves at Tor House, by the Chalice Well in 1886, starting a boys' school. They were followed in 1903 by the Sisters of Charity of St Louis who purchased the Priory building (now next door to St Mary's) in Magdalene Street, starting an orphanage, and later, a primary school.

So, after a period of 347 years, the first regular Catholic clergy took up residence again in Glastonbury, and on 21st September 1886, the first public Holy Mass was celebrated. The first Catholic Baptism to be recorded was 20th October 1888. The Missionaries' chapel was now the nascent focal point for those few Catholics of Glastonbury, estimated by a Fr Gouffe in 1892, "at about thirty, none of any standing, except one influential family, the Bisgoods".

Recusant pilgrims, singly or in small clandestine groups, made their journey to Glastonbury, as pilgrims did and had done to Jerusalem, Rome, Santiago de

Compostela, Canterbury, throughout the ages, in spite of wars, prohibition or pestilence. What must have been the return of the first, formal public pilgrimage, led by the Bishop of Clifton, with the Abbot and monks of Downside Abbey, was on the 12th of September 1895. According to the *Daily Telegraph*: "The procession comprised upwards of 100 Ecclesiastics of all degrees... distinguished lay members... several prominent members of the Catholic Truth Society, and in addition, 1100 ladies and gentlemen from various parts of England.... Its slow, toilsome march ascending the narrow counterscarp of the Tor... was a striking sight, full of moral significance, as well as imposing effect... ."

Today, this major pilgrimage tradition still takes place every year, centred round the Abbey, with Anglicans and Catholics holding their respective pilgrimages during the summer. Both are major events in the Town, and well supported by the Town officials. Of course, there are also many other, smaller pilgrim groups and individuals who travel to Glastonbury round the year from this country and many other parts of the world.

And in another demonstration of the significant influence that the Abbey holds in connection with Our Lady, was that of the twelve-year-old heiress, Charlotte Boyd, wandering the ruins of the Abbey in 1850, vividly imagining this great place at its height in the Middle Ages. Subsequently, amongst her other restoration projects of religious buildings, she purchased in 1896 the neglected fourteenth century Slipper Chapel just outside Walsingham, Norfolk, another prominent mediaeval Marian pilgrimage destination. The restored Slipper Chapel formed the nucleus of the now National Shrine to Our Lady in England. Two years after the first Glastonbury pilgrimage described above, the first organised post-Reformation pilgrimage was made to Walsingham.

The parish churches

When the Missionaries of the Sacred Heart closed their school, leaving for Ireland in 1913, the Sisters' convent chapel now took up service for the embryonic parish, until, in 1926, a stable block on the convent property was converted into a small church, becoming in effect, the first parish church, seating about fifty.

On Sunday 5th December 1926, Fr Francis Burdett, the first parish priest, having been deputed by the Bishop of Clifton to bless this small chapel, celebrated the first Mass there. He remarked poignantly, "that from this church, as from the stable where the Incarnation took place, the Catholic community might work a change in Glastonbury, just as the Incarnation changed the whole world".

Adorning the chapel was a 75cm-high statue of the Madonna and Child, commissioned by Fr Burdett, and carved in Portland stone by the eminent sculptor Eric

The convent stable - the first parish church.

Gill. By circuitous routes, following the demolition of the chapel in 1938, this valuable and precious statue, in the custody of Clifton Diocese, is now on display at the visitor centre of Glastonbury Abbey.

In March 1938, a young curate, Fr Michael Fitzpatrick, from St Mary's, Bath, was charged by the Bishop with the raising and building of a new parish church on a plot on the convent grounds gifted by the Sisters. Building started in 1939, and despite wartime constraints, it was completed, and opened in July 1940, at a total cost of £11,000.

The new church was consecrated and dedicated to Our Lady St Mary of Glastonbury on 2nd July 1941, on the Feast of the Visitation, by the Bishop of Clifton. Parishioners, as they left the church through the narthex doors - as they do now - can look across directly into the Abbey grounds, where stands the Lady Chapel of the Great Abbey - the new was at last reconnected with the old.

Meditation - "Arise Mary…"

"Arise, Mary, and go forth in the strength into that north country, which was once thy own, and take possession of a land which knows thee not. Arise, Mother of God, and with thy thrilling voice, speak to those who labour with child, and are in pain, till the babe of grace leaps within them! Shine on us, dear Lady, with thy bright countenance, like the sun in his strength, *O Stella matutina*, O Harbinger of Peace, till our year is one perpetual May... O Mary, my hope, O Mother undefiled, fulfill to us the promise of this Spring."

Blessed John Henry Newman,
sermon, *The Second Spring*

Shrine and Coronation

In 1955, this humble, country parish church was canonically restored as a Shrine. The Apostolic Delegate blessed a statue of Our Lady, thereby returning it, and the Shrine, to the ancient title of 'Our Lady St Mary of Glastonbury'. The statue was sculpted by Philip Lindsey Clark FRBS from a depiction of Our Lady shown in a fourteenth century seal from the Abbey.

Ten years later, on the 4th of July 1965, in what was described by the presiding Apostolic Delegate as the 'greatest religious event since the Reformation', took place, with the statue of Our Lady of Glastonbury being solemnly crowned with a crown of gold fashioned from melted jewelry donated by parishioners. As a gracious symbol of unity the Anglican Bishop of Bath and Wells offered the Abbey grounds for the ceremony, as well as attending in a place of honour. Over 20,000 people were present.

As proclaimed by the Apostolic Delegate during the Pontifical Mass:

"It is the first time that Catholics and Anglicans join as brothers in a solemn act of filial devotion to the Mother of Christ on the spot where she was first invoked, as Our Lady St Mary of Glastonbury. There is no doubt that this celebration is the greatest event that has ever happened in Glastonbury since the unity of the Christian body was broken in these lands".

"A new era of Christian history is now in the making, old rivalries have given way to a new spirit of charity. As the role of Our Lady in the plan of Redemption is more fully understood, may we not hope that this restored Shrine may under God's Providence play an important part in uniting God's children in one family again."

Fr J Macnamara,
Parish Priest at the Shrine's Silver Jubilee, 1966

In 1984, the convent of St Louis closed, with the original Priory House building, immediately next door to St Mary's, latterly being converted to private housing.

So, this modest, modern church had now taken on the mantle of being the oldest Marian Shrine in northern Europe. The communications and travel opportunities of the modern age have given it a truly international dimension, judging by the number and world-wide origins of the many pilgrims and visitors that come to the Shrine, and by the number of prayer requests made from all over the world on the Shrine's website petition page.

The Restored Shrine

The church is set back from Magdalene Street, fronted by a small rustic, flag-stoned forecourt. In outward appearance it is a sturdy, bluff church, built of rough-faced quarry stone. It has a pleasing, simple symmetry, with an elegant, high Gothic arch on the front façade, and slim, elegant, full-length delicately arched windows down the sides.

On entry to the narthex, your eyes are immediately drawn through the double '*Alpha and Omega*' inscribed glass doors, right down the nave, to the Shrine. For there, at the end of the sanctuary, behind the altar and high up, stands the graceful, crowned statue of Our Lady of Glastonbury, demurely presenting her infant Son to the world.

Once inside the church, you get an impression of light, height and space, and clean, minimal lines. Plain crisp, white walls, a profusion of those slender, full length stippled plain-glass windows, and polished parquet-tiled floor, all add to this impression.

Having seen the statue of Our Lady, your first inclination may now be to head down the nave to kneel and give thanks to Jesus present in the Blessed Sacrament, at the place of honour in the gleaming brass tabernacle just behind the altar. Here, you will see on the column between statue and tabernacle, the perfect combination, wholly summated by the crisp, gold letters 'IESVS MARIA' carved on a stone taken from the Abbey ruins

Benediction at the Shrine of Our Lady of Glastonbury.

and presented by their Trustees - a haunting echo and replication of that ancient inscription carved so lovingly, on the south wall of the Abbey's Lady Chapel.

"If we wish to discover in all its richness the profound relationship between the Church and the Eucharist, we cannot neglect Mary, Mother and model of the Church... Mary can guide us toward this most holy sacrament, because she herself has a profound relationship with it."

Blessed Pope John Paul II,
Ecclesia de Eucharistia

Pilgrim's Prayer

Dear loving Lord Jesus, as pilgrim and sojourner on my earthly journey, I thank you so much for leading me by your own purpose, to this holy place.

I kneel before you in praise, thanksgiving and adoration.

I pray before your Holy Mother for the grace of faith to discern your purpose, and that you may "grant my heart's desire, and fulfill every one of my plans" (cf. *Ps* 20:4).

I pray, that inspired by the witness of those countless pilgrims who, with their faith, have also passed through this town throughout the centuries, and, by the sacrifice of your holy martyrs who gave their lives for this faith, that I too may be faithful and live my life by your holy will.

I pray for perseverance to continue on my life's journey with the steadfastness and commitment that you took on your journey to Calvary.

I pray for the hope of the Resurrection, and rejoice in the knowledge, that by faithfully treading my pilgrim path on earth, will surely lead me to the Heavenly Jerusalem.

I humbly pray for the people of this Parish, and this town, and all others who come here, that the Truth they seek is yours.

I turn to you, O Mary of Glastonbury, to bestow your motherly love and protection, and watch over me while I continue my journey.

I pray also for all those, who in their time of need, have left their petitions before you in this, your holy Shrine, and for your intercession before your Beloved Son.

I lay before you my own petitions for your gracious intercession....

Hail Mary... Our Father.... Glory be....

The statue and tapestry

You may now start to take note of what is going on around you in more detail. The statue itself, with Our Lady robed in the vibrant, rich colours of royalty: crimson, gold and blue; the child Jesus's hand raised in blessing, and in Our Lady's right hand a stem of white roses - that eternal sign of love. She is sheltered by the surrounding willow-weave hurdles, in green and gold metalwork, so redolent an artifact of the Levels of Somerset. In all, a most graceful and evocative image.

Next, the large tapestry left and right of the statue, forming the *reredos*. On the left, the five figures you see are taken from the history of Glastonbury, on the right, from legend and tradition.

Bottom left, in his bishop's cope and mitre of red and gold, is St Dunstan, who whilst gazing up at Our Lady, is rather disdainfully and effortlessly grasping the devil by his nostrils with a pair of pincers. This is the great St Dunstan: reviver of monasticism, distinguished Abbot of Glastonbury Abbey, Archbishop of Canterbury.

In front of St Dunstan, kneeling, is the Carthusian monk, Blessed Richard Bere, Glastonbury-born nephew of Abbot Bere. With nine other Carthusians he was starved to death at Newgate Prison, London, in 1536, for refusing to take Henry VIII's Oath of Supremacy. The two Benedictine monks above St Dunstan are Roger James (Sacrist) and John Thorne (Abbey Treasurer), both martyred alongside their Abbot. And lastly, the elderly Abbot, Blessed Richard Whiting, with his Abbot's cross and crosier, offering up the instrument of his death, the hangman's noose.

From the right-hand tapestry: at the bottom, kneeling is St Brigid, the Irish Saint born c453 near Dundalk, and foundress of the monastic life for women in Ireland.

Tradition has it that she made pilgrimage to Glastonbury in 488, staying in nearby Beckery ('little Eire') on the western side of Glastonbury, where there is tantalising evidence of a small oratory. She is portrayed as an energetic, generous woman, as equally at home tending to the sick, or at her milking stool - which is how she is depicted here, with her cow by her side and her stool in her hand.

Immediately above her is St Patrick, in his shamrock-emblazoned cope, holding aloft his 'trademark' cross *pattée*, proclaiming his Christian faith. There is tell in ancient legend that St Patrick returned to Britain in his old age, and at Glastonbury, with some local hermits, founded the fledgling abbey.

And then, St David, said to have come to Glastonbury as a pilgrim in 530 to bless 'a monastery which was becoming famous in the Celtic world'. He is shown with a white dove in his hand, commemorating the occasion when it is said that a white dove alighted on him when he was preaching.

Lastly, Joseph of Arimathea, about whom much has already been said in this booklet. Here, holding his staff as the Holy Thorn in his right hand, and the blazing Holy Grail in his left.

This vibrant, beautifully composed and executed tapestry was designed by Brother Louis Barlow of the Benedictine Abbey at Prinknash, Gloucestershire. It was woven by the Edinburgh Tapestry Company Ltd, taking five weavers 240 working hours to complete, employing a craft unchanged for some 3,000 years, being woven by hand on an upright loom. It took place of honour, flanking Our Lady, when the statue was re-installed in the Shrine after her coronation in 1965.

The church

Above the statue is the elegant trio of stained glass windows of the Calvary scene. The setting sun, when shining directly through this window, surrounds the Crucified One in a glorious blaze of golden light. The bottom left-hand panel shows St Dunstan and the coat of arms of the Clifton Diocese. The centre section shows the signing of the Charter by King Ine of Wessex, and on the right is Blessed Richard Whiting and the coat of arms of the Mostyn family, who gifted the windows.

Down by the altar rail, on the right hand side in a glass case, is the Shrine petitions book, for visitors and pilgrims to kneel at and pray for those who have sought Our Lady's intercession. Petitioners not only have the reassurance of these pilgrim prayers, but the regular prayers of parishioners, and the offerings made at every Mass in the Shrine.

In the right hand (north) transept, is a portrait of the Blessed Richard Whiting, gazing up at the place of his death, the Tor. Below him is the illuminated, approved copy of the Glastonbury Prayer (see below), and the authorisation from the Holy See of the crowning of the statue of Our Lady of Glastonbury.

Stepping further back you will see the two simple, arched side chapels, on the left to St Joseph, and on the right, the Sacred Heart. Moving further back down the church you will notice halfway down on the left, the wooden carved statue of St Anthony of Padua, presented by the prominent Italian community who were initially brought to Glastonbury as prisoners of war, working in the area, and subsequently settling and marrying into the local community.

If you are staying a while, we offer some prayers and meditations for you:

The Glastonbury Prayers

"O Lord Jesus Christ, whose glorious Mother was honoured for so many centuries under the title of Our Lady St Mary of Glastonbury, grant that through her intercession, together with that of your blessed martyrs, Richard Whiting, Roger James and John Thorne, who in Glastonbury laid down their lives for their Faith, that true unity of Faith may be restored among Christians in this country, and that your servants may ever rejoice in health of mind and body, to render you fitting service. Amen.

At this Shrine of our Blessed Lady, we ask you, Almighty Father, to fill our hearts with thanks for our redemption; and as the names of Jesus and Mary were linked together in Glastonbury's ancient shrine, we confidently ask, through the merits of your divine Son and the intercession of his blessed Mother, that you will grant us all we need for soul and body. Amen."

Prayer for England

"O blessed Virgin Mary, Mother of God and our most gentle Queen and Mother, look down in mercy upon England thy Dowry, and upon us all who greatly hope and trust in thee. By thee it was that Jesus, our Saviour and our Hope, was given unto the world, and he has given thee to us that we may hope still more. Plead for us thy children, whom thou didst receive and accept at the foot of the cross, O sorrowful Mother. Intercede for our separated brethren, that with us in the one true fold, they may be united to the Chief Shepherd, the Vicar of thy Son. Pray for us all, dear Mother, that by faith fruitful in good works, we may all deserve to see and praise God, together with thee, in our heavenly home.

Our Lady of Glastonbury - pray for us."

Rosary recommendation: The Joyful Mysteries: the Annunciation, the Visitation, the Nativity of the Lord, the Presentation in the Temple, and, the Finding in the Temple. If circumstance precludes, pray the fourth decade - the Presentation - just as here Our Lady presents the Lord, in this his temple, to us - and the world.

Meditation - "...meeting with Mary..."

"Pilgrimages are very often the way to enter the tent of meeting with Mary, the Mother of the Lord. Mary, in whom the pilgrimage of the Word towards humankind converges with humankind's pilgrimage of faith, thus becoming the 'star of evangelisation' for the journey of the whole Church... Her womb was the first shrine, the tent of meeting between Divinity and humanity... The Magnificat then becomes the song par excellence, not only of the pilgrimage of Mary, but also our pilgrimage in hope."

The Pilgrimage in the Great Jubilee.

The Tor

"In our own time the price to be paid for fidelity to the Gospel is no longer to be hanged, drawn and quartered, but it often involves being dismissed out of hand, ridiculed, or parodied. And yet, the Church cannot withdraw from the task of proclaiming Christ and his Gospel as saving truth, the source of our ultimate happiness as individuals, and as the foundation of a just and Christian society."

Pope Benedict XVI addressing the Hyde Park Vigil during his state visit to Britain in 2010.

Despite being a relatively small feature - a diminutive 518 feet high - the Tor can be spotted from afar in many parts of Somerset. This is made possible not only by its distinct conical shape, topped by a blunt, stone tower, but also with its relative prominence, rising up from the surrounding low-lying Somerset Levels.

'Tor' is a local West country word meaning 'rocky-topped hill' or crag. Its hard cap of sandstone has resisted erosion in comparison to its surrounds, giving the height and distinct shape. This little hill distinguished itself before the watching world - albeit unwittingly - as one of the prominent features of the opening ceremony of the 2012 London Olympic Games.

Fact and myth

Excavations around the top of the Tor have revealed evidence of human occupation during the Dark Ages; Neolithic flint tools have been discovered, as well as Roman remains. Through skeletal remains there is evidence of a Saxon hermitage, which would have been a daughter house of the monastery below. Later a church, dedicated to St Michael, took its place, which was destroyed by the earthquake that hit the South of England in 1275. A second church was built in the 1360s, until its destruction during the Dissolution - leaving just the present tower standing proud. The tower is a Grade I listed building, and the Tor area is National Trust property, with free access.

As well as geology and archaeology telling us the facts about the Tor, as ever with all things Glastonbury, it tells much else in mysticism and legend. It is held to have been a sacred place for the Iron Age Celts of those ancient lake villages. It is said to be positioned on prominent ley lines - hypothetical alignments that cross through ancient sacred sites, attributed with having special energy and cosmic power. Other myths tell of the Tor being the entrance to the underworld, or there being a cave deep inside, or part of a gigantic aerial zodiac, or the site of a sacred, ancient maze. The seven, deep, roughly symmetrical terraces wrapping round the Tor are also a source of speculation: were they for cultivation purposes, or cut by countless hooves of grazing animals; defensive ramparts, or part of an ancient, three-dimensional labyrinth?

In the Middle Ages, two week-long fairs were held each September on the lower slopes of the Tor - remembered by the present name 'Fairfield'. The earliest was granted by Henry I in 1126, being held on the Nativity of the Blessed Virgin, when "a host of pilgrims used to assemble to celebrate [what] appears to have been the chief festival observed at [Mary's] shrine", and thus perhaps kept as "the feast of Our Lady of Glastonbury". The other fair held at *the monastery of St Michael de Torre*' which culminated at Michaelmas, was granted by Henry III in 1243.

For Christians, it is a place to recollect where prayer held sway for many centuries within this hilltop church, and for Catholics, it is the sombre setting for martyrdom - for here, in front of the church tower on this windswept hill with its sweeping, panoramic views, was the place of martyrdom for the Abbot of Glastonbury, Blessed Richard Whiting, and two of his monks, Blessed Roger James and Blessed John Thorne.

Walking and praying

The Tor is easily walkable from the town, taking twenty-five minutes or so. There are two principal routes, the noisier, but more direct A361/Chilkwell Street heading out of town, which leads you up past the Rural Life Museum and Chalice Well, through Fairfields and up the

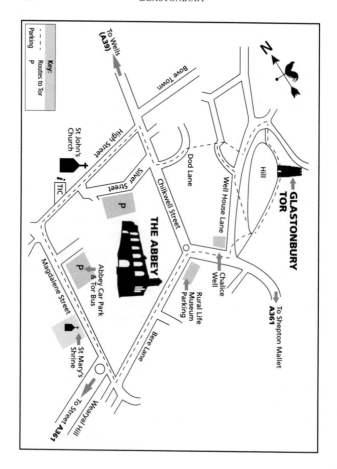

longer spine of the Tor; or up Dod Lane (off Lambrook Street), the quieter route across the fields above the town, leading to the northern entrance, with the more direct approach up the face of the Tor. You can, of course, walk this whole route as a circuit. There is very limited disabled car parking (only) at this entrance; a park and ride scheme operates in the summer season from the Abbey car park.

> **Rosary recommendation:** As you walk, pray the Sorrowful Mysteries: The Agony in the Garden, the Scourging at the Pillar, the Crowning with Thorns, the Carrying of the Cross, the Crucifixion and Death of Jesus. If time or circumstance preclude, consider praying the fifth decade at the top of the Tor - the Crucifixion.

After your short toil to the top, you will be rewarded by the glorious, 360 degree panoramic views, which on a clear day are extensive. The mottled, weathered tower, although standing foursquare between its sturdy, stepped buttresses, also shows touches of elegance with its Gothic arched entrances, statue niches and crenellated crown.

A compass plinth indicates all the prominent places and features to view: to the north, the city of Wells, and the two blunt towers of the cathedral; looking westwards, the glint of the Bristol Channel and the shadow of the Welsh hills beyond; and then the Somerset coastline, with its seaside towns, and the distinct cubes of Hinkley nuclear power station, which lead on up to the soft Quantock hills; south west and close to, the town of Street, and just below you, Wearyall Hill; round to the south on the near skyline, in the gap between trees, the slender column of the Admiral Hood monument, then the pointed steeple of Kingweston church; and round to the east, the folly at Stourhead, Alfred's Tower.

At the summit, in front of the tower, looking down onto Glastonbury and the Abbey, you may wish, individually or as a group, to make an **Act of Remembrance of the Glastonbury Martyrs**, with these readings and prayers:

Readings

Romans 5:1-5

"So then, now that we have been justified by faith, we are at peace with God through our Lord Jesus Christ; it is through him, by faith, that we have been admitted into God's favour in which we are living, and look forward exultantly to God's glory. Not only that; let us exult, too, in our hardships, understanding that hardship develops perseverance, and perseverance develops a tested character, something that gives us hope, and a hope which will not let us down, because the love of God has been poured into our hearts by the Holy Spirit which has been given to us."

Psalm 3:3,4,5,8

"R. Into your hands Lord, I commend my spirit.

You, Yahweh, the shield at my side, my glory,
you hold my head high.
I cry out to Yahweh;
   he answers from his holy mountain. **R.**
As for me, if I lie down and sleep, I shall awake,
   for Yahweh sustains me. **R.**
In Yahweh is salvation, on your people, your blessing! **R."**

Matthew 16:24-26

"Then Jesus said to his disciples, 'If anyone wants to be a follower of mine, let him renounce himself and take up his cross and follow me. Anyone who wants to save his life will lose it; but anyone who loses his life for my sake will find it. What, then, will anyone gain by winning the whole world and forfeiting his life? Or what can anyone offer in exchange for his life?'"

Meditation: I shall take the cup of salvation

"Of this cup the martyrs said: *I shall take the cup of salvation and call upon the name of the Lord.*

But are you not afraid you will weaken?

No, they reply.

And why? Because I shall call upon the name of the Lord. Do you think martyrs could have been victorious, unless he was victorious in the martyrs who said:

Rejoice, for I have overcome the world?

The Lord of the heavens directed their minds and tongues; through them he overcame the devil on earth and crowned them as martyrs in heaven.

Blessed are those who have drunk of this cup!

Their torments are at an end, and they have taken their place of honour.

And so, my dear ones, consider: although you cannot see with your eyes, do so with your mind and soul, and see that the death of the saints is precious in the sight of the Lord."

From a sermon by St Augustine of Hippo
- The Martyr's Cup of Suffering

Prayers

"Our Saviour's faithfulness is mirrored in the fidelity of his witnesses who shed their blood for the Word of God. Let us praise him in remembrance of them:

You redeemed us by your blood.

Your martyrs freely embraced death in bearing witness for the faith - give us the true freedom of the Spirit, O Lord.

You redeemed us by your blood.

Your martyrs professed their faith by shedding their blood - give us a faith, O Lord, that is constant and pure.

You redeemed us by your blood.

Your martyrs followed in your footstep by carrying the Cross - help us to endure courageously the misfortunes of life.

You redeemed us by your blood.

Your martyrs washed their garments in the blood of the Lamb - help us to avoid the weaknesses of the flesh and worldly allurements.

You redeemed us by your blood.

All powerful, ever living God, you gave Blesseds Richard Whiting, Roger James and John Thorne the courage to witness to the gospel of Christ, even to the point of giving their lives for it. By their prayers help us to endure all suffering for love of you and to seek you with all our hearts, for you alone are the source of life. Grant this through our Lord Jesus Christ, your Son, who lives and reigns with you and the Holy Spirit, one God, for ever and ever. Amen."

"I have fought the good fight to the end; I have run the race to the finish; I have kept the faith; all there is to come for me now is the crown of uprightness which the Lord, the upright judge, will give to me on that day; and not only to me but to all those who have longed for his appearing."

2 Tm 4:7-8

Other Places of Interest

Estate buildings of the Abbey:

Abbey Gatehouse: Built in mid-fourteenth century, now houses administrative offices.

The Tribunal: High Street. A mediaeval merchant's house built late fifteenth century, also attributed as the Abbot's Court House. It is now the **Tourist Information Centre** and Glastonbury Lake Village Museum.

George and Pilgrim Inn: High Street. 'Overflow accommodation' for pilgrims from the Abbot's guest quarters, late fifteenth century. Now an atmospheric pub/hotel.

Rural Life Museum: Bere Lane (en route to the Tor). Fourteenth century tithe barn used to store Abbey estates' produce and tithes. As a museum it presents fine displays of social and agricultural histories of Somerset.

In and around Glastonbury:

The Church of St John the Baptist: High Street. This imposing, welcoming fifteenth century Anglican church in the centre of town is well worth a visit. Holy Thorns grow in the churchyard, and there is a labyrinth. The magnificent tower is the second tallest of parish churches in Somerset.

Inside you will be struck by the loft of the central nave, which is lit at the upper level by clerestory windows. Your eye is drawn to the expanse of the intricately detailed stained glass window at the back of the sanctuary. In the north (left hand) transept is a striking portrayal of Joseph of Arimathea in stained glass. Also displayed here is a funeral pall made in 1774 from a cope traditionally worn by Abbot Whiting. Two very unusual and arresting statues - Resurrection Christ and the Madonna and Child are at the back, carved in wood by Ernst Blensdorf, a refugee from Nazism. St George's chapel in the south transept is reserved for quiet prayer.

St Benedict's Church: Benedict Street. A church has been on this site since 1100, with the present church being built in 1520 by Abbot Bere. It displays the perpendicular style, with a clerestoried nave, and in the tradition of Somerset churches, presents a fine tower.

Other churches in Glastonbury: Methodist Church, Lambrook Street; United Reform Church, High Street; Grace Community Church, Wirral Park.

St Margaret's Chapel (and Magdalene Almshouses): Off Magdalene Street. Built in 1444 as a hospital and later as an almshouse. A calm, peaceful place with a small chapel and diminutive, neat garden.

The Glastonbury Millennium Trail: A circular route round the town taking in the above, and more. Starts at the Town Hall going in a clockwise direction. Pavement markers and information boards will keep you on track. It takes about an hour. Explanatory pamphlet available from the Tourist Information Office.

Pilgrim Reception Centre: 10b High Street. Reflecting the huge diversity of seekers coming to contemporary Glastonbury, the volunteer-manned Centre handles enquiries from the widest range of beliefs, faiths, and paths.

Chalice Well and Gardens: Chilkwell Street (en route to the Tor): Site of an ancient and natural wellspring, with close associations with the Glastonbury legends, set in peaceful, extensive and well-tended gardens with interesting features. It is also where the Missionaries of the Sacred Heart settled, re-establishing the Catholic Church in Glastonbury, although their buildings are long gone.

Wearyall Hill: Hill feature just west of the Tor, where by legend Joseph of Arimathea planted his staff. Easily walkable from the town. Here you will see the vandalised stump of the 1951 Holy Thorn alongside the latest re-planting, and a good view across to the Tor.

Beckery Chapel: (field just off Morlands Road, Morlands Enterprise Park). All that can be seen now is the small hillock, Bride's Mound, and two explanatory boards, where stood a small late thirteenth century stone chapel owned by the Abbey, and is the site associated by legend with St Brigid's Oratory (fifth century).

Baltonsborough: St Dunstan is commemorated in the nearby village of his birth, Baltonsborough, by the sturdy fifteenth century church named after him, with its simple, square, Somerset tower. It is set in a tranquil village location by a mill stream.

Stratton-on-the-Fosse:

Downside Abbey: About fifteen miles from Glastonbury is the imposing neo-Gothic Benedictine Abbey Church of St Gregory the Great, with its distinctive tower. It is described as, "The most splendid demonstration of the renaissance of Roman Catholicism in England". After the Reformation, exiled English Catholics founded a Benedictine House in Douai, France, in 1607, sending monks back to England on the 'English mission', during which six were martyred. The community was expelled from France in 1795 during the Revolution, arriving at Downside, via Shropshire, in 1814. Building started in 1873, finally being completed in 1925. Although supporting a large, busy school, the timeless monastic life continues, with the daily liturgy being celebrated by the monks, for which the Abbey church is open to those who wish to attend. There is a pastoral centre and bookshop with a welcoming café.

Wells:

Wells Cathedral: "The most poetic of English cathedrals" - glorious twelfth century Gothic cathedral largely unaffected by the Reformation. Famous for its unique inverted 'scissor' arch, fourteenth century 'jousting clock', iconic Chapter house and peaceful cloisters. There is also a lovely Lady chapel.

Bishop's Palace: Beautiful mediaeval palace and extensive gardens open to the public. Site of the wellsprings from which the town is named after, and the ruins of the Great Hall in which Abbot Whiting was tried. Famous for its moat and resident swans.

St Cuthbert's Church: The largest Anglican parish church in Somerset, sometimes mistaken for the Cathedral. With its origins from twelfth century, it has an amazing carved and decorated sixteenth century ceiling in the Nave.

Select Reading List

Ashe, Geoffrey, *King Arthur's Avalon; the Story of Glastonbury* (1957, re-published 2007).

Carley, James P., *Glastonbury Abbey: The Holy House at the Head of the Moors Adventurous* (1996).

Dunning, Robert, *Glastonbury: History and Guide* (1994).

Hopkinson-Ball, T F *Glastonbury Origins of the Sacred.*